Contents

Teaching Guide

Specific answers are given as part of this guide. There will be some instances where the answers could vary. If a student has an answer that is reasonable, accept it. The idea of these word puzzles is not only to increase the students' vocabularies, but to also increase their reasoning skills.

Answer Key

Page 1
1. "Oh, I see you are empty!"
2. "You are a beauty!"
3. "You are a cutie!"
4. "I see you!"
5. "Are you okay?"
6. "You are easy!"
7. "I see T.V.!"
8. "You are A-OK!"

Page 2
1. eye
2. hand
3. paddles
4. sun
5. bear
6. fence
7. bird
8. foot
9. tree
10. daughter

Page 3
See page.

Page 4
1 to jack rabbit
2 to chameleon
3 to skunk
4 to turtle
5 to porcupine
6 to jellyfish
7 to armadillo
8 to octopus
9 to puffer
10 to opossum

Page 5
Across
1. Michigan
3. Kansas
6. Idaho
7. Oklahoma
8. Utah
9. Alabama

Down
1. Missouri
2. Montana
4. Florida
5. Iowa
7. Ohio

Page 6

```
F L I N N M R C C O P
E A M P S H L R O N T
W I T E P E A D R M R
A M O C C A S I N S A
M O C C A D S K I N R
P R E S E D S K I T R
U N D E R R A S P E O
M T E P E E A R T S W
T M Y X L S P E A R S
P A P O O S E R S E D
```

Page 6 (cont.)
1. headdress
2. Moccasins
3. tepee
4. corn
5. Wampum
6. papoose
7. skin
8. arrows
9 spear

Page 7
1. lungs
2. stomach
3. heart
4. tongue
5. ear
6. rib
7. brain
8. nose
9. eyes
10. skin

Page 8
1. halfback
2. snowball
3. notebook
4. peanut
5. baseball
6. fishhook
7. cowboy
8. cardboard
9. pigpen
10. sunburn
See page for matching.

Page 9
Across
3. after
4. thirty
7. before
9. ten

Down
1. past
2. quarter
5. hour
6. to
8. one

Page 10
1. bat
2. ball
3. base
4. kick
5. pop
6. goal
7. basketball
8. set
9. feet
10. you

Page 11

Page 12

1 to sink
2 to bark
3 to spoke
4 to nail
5 to track
6 to note
7 to spade
8 to top
9 to shade
10 to litter

Page 13

Across
6. bee
7. giraffe
8. dog
10. zebra
11. penguin

Down
1. snake
2. frog
3. tiger
4. calf
5. bird
6. buffalo
9. gorilla

Page 14

Across
1. drops
3. Clouds
6. rain
8. oceans

Down
2. snow
3. cooler
4. shape
5. wind
7. low

Page 15

1. pair to pear
2. peace to piece
3. four to for
4. meet to meat
5. one to won
6. tail to tale
7. buy to by
8. two to too
9. weak to week
10. dear to deer

Page 16

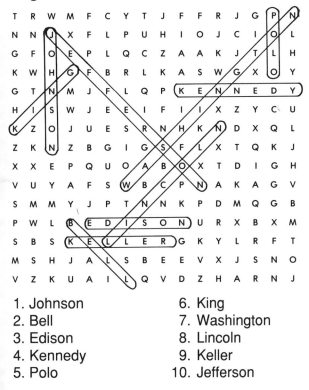

1. Johnson
2. Bell
3. Edison
4. Kennedy
5. Polo
6. King
7. Washington
8. Lincoln
9. Keller
10. Jefferson

Page 17

1. rabbit
2. fox
3. bee
4. glass
5. clouds
6. roses
7. ax
8. bear
9. turtle
10. mouse

Page 18

2. (across) butterfly
3. (down) egg
7. (down) plants
4. (down) larva
6. (across) caterpillar
5. (across) growing
8. (across) spins
1. (down) pupa
9. (across) shell
6. (down) changes

Page 19

1. elephant
2. plate
3. eight
4. cold
5. walk
6. scales
7. Music
8. banana
9. fruit
10. blue

Page 20

Across
1. black
4. minister
6. was
7. peace

Down
1. born
2. Alabama
3. rights
5. schools
6. won
8. equal

Page 21

1. cap
2. present
3. carpet
4. look
5. place
6. small
7. large
8. noisy
9. ocean
10. halt
11. seat
12. glass

Page 22

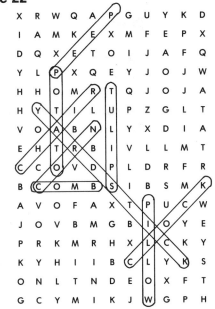

Word Puzzles

Page 22 (cont.)
1. chair
2. potato
3. tulips
4. clock
5. comb
6. corn
7. yardstick
8. peep
9. pillow

Page 23

Across
3. Jupiter
4. Earth
7. Saturn
8. planet
9. orbit

Down
1. Pluto
2. nine
5. hot
6. Mercury
7. sun

Page 24

Across
2. smile
3. tender
6. lint
8. rind
9. mirror
10. wade

Down
1. slit
2. squirm
4. narrow
5. reduce
7. tired

Page 25

sail	ant	dew
sale	aunt	do
pale	tail	blue
pail	tale	blew
so	scent	whole
sew	cent	hole
sun	ate	hare
son	eight	hair
eye	heard	hear
I	herd	here

Page 26

Across
1. globe
5. south
6. west
7. Pole
9. part

Down
2. left
3. east
4. ice
6. water
8. top
10. land

Page 27

```
V U W G Y F J N B X Y E G G
I C J H N X B R F Z N Q O Z
F R M L M D I G Z M R B G A
H X X Q A Y A I K V P R Z C
W K L C P N D T T B D S H A
E A S U J D G A R D E N E R
Y M Z M Z G Y R Y O N Z X D
D D Q D C Z O S Y D U S H C
L G E O D X M O Z K R B Z S
I B J H U U Y L Z O T E L V
S R U O L Q L Y W P E M A E
W A T C H U D Y P R M J U M
V V D X H Z H X I Q Z E D A
G E C J V Z Y B U L I M E W
```

1. brave
2. clumsy
3. dizzy
4. gardener
5. trouble
6. angry
7. watch
8. sad
9. daydream

Page 28

Across
2. hour
3. dogs
4. summer
5. ocean

Down
1. tree
2. high
3. drive
4. supper
6. cut

| | | E | Z | 2 | C | | (E | A | S | Y | | T | O | | S | E | E | !) | | | |

Single letters and numbers are used for words in the following sentences.
Rewrite the sentences using words.

1. When Mother Hubbard went to the cupboard, she said,

"O, I C U R M T!"

_____

_____

2. Your mother is lovely. In letters you might say,

"U R A B U T!"

_____

_____

3. Your uncle looked at your baby brother and said,

"U R A Q T!"

_____

_____

4. One of the children playing Hide and Seek said,

"I C U!"

_____

_____

5. One of your friends looks pale. You ask,

"R U O K?"

_____

_____

6. When a child finished his homework, he said,

"U R E Z!"

_____

_____

7. The baby pulled herself up in front of the television and said,

"I C T V!"

_____

_____

8. When one friend finished helping another, he said,

"U R A O K!"

_____

_____

Word Puzzles

1

ANALOGIES

Cut out the picture and paste it where it belongs. Write the word pictured on the blank.

1. Hear is to ear as see is to _____.

2. Leg is to foot as arm is to _____.

3. Car is to motor as rowboat is to _____.

4. Night is to moon as day is to _____.

5. Calf is to cow as cub is to _____.

6. Door is to house as gate is to _____.

7. Fur is to squirrel as feather is to _____.

8. Finger is to hand as toe is to _____.

9. Flower is to plant as leaf is to _____.

10. Father is to son as mother is to _____.

Word Puzzles

2

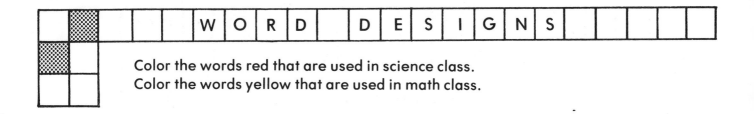

W O R D   D E S I G N S

Color the words red that are used in science class.
Color the words yellow that are used in math class.

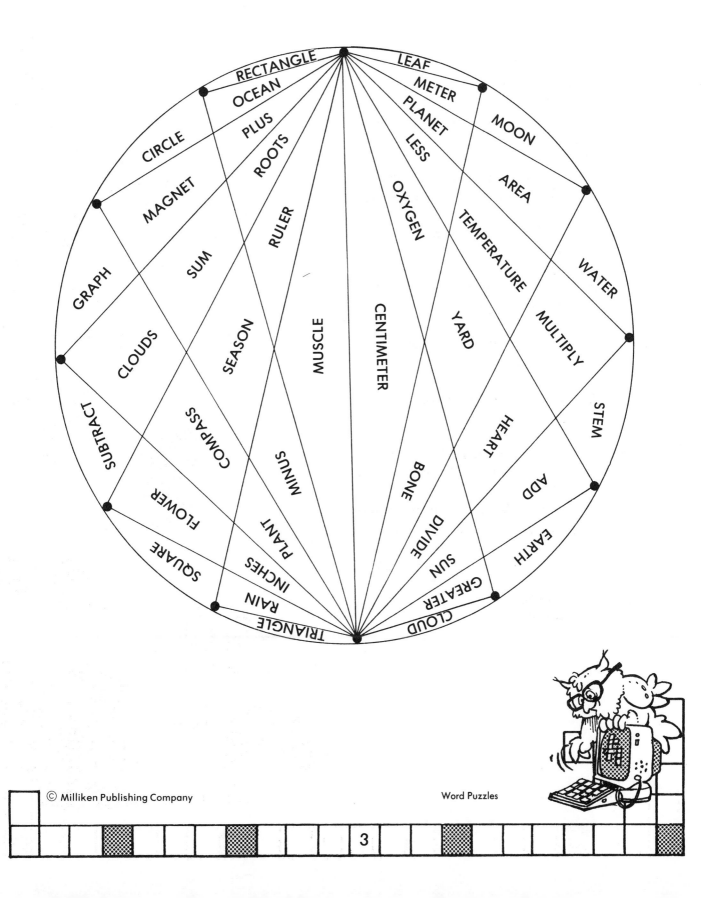

RECTANGLE · LEAF · OCEAN · METER · PLANET · MOON · CIRCLE · PLUS · ROOTS · LESS · AREA · MAGNET · RULER · OXYGEN · TEMPERATURE · WATER · SUM · GRAPH · SEASON · MUSCLE · CENTIMETER · YARD · MULTIPLY · CLOUDS · COMPASS · MINUS · BONE · HEART · STEM · SUBTRACT · FLOWER · PLANT · DIVIDE · ADD · INCHES · SUN · EARTH · SQUARE · RAIN · TRIANGLE · CLOUD · GREATER

ANIMALS PROTECT THEMSELVES

Draw a line to match the animals with the sentences.

jellyfish

skunk

puffer

jack rabbit

chameleon

turtle

porcupine

opossum

armadillo

octopus

1. The coat of this white-tailed hare turns completely white in the winter.

2. This lizard can change color to match his surroundings.

3. This black and white animal gives off a very bad smell which sends its enemies away.

4. This animal protects itself by pulling its head in its shell.

5. The sharp, painful quills on this animal protect it from its enemies.

6. This fish looks like a floating umbrella and shoots out poison threads.

7. This animal rolls itself into a tight ball inside its shell.

8. This animal squirts a black liquid into the water so its enemies cannot see it.

9. This fish blows itself up like a balloon and becomes too big for an enemy to hold.

10. When in danger, this animal pretends it is dead.

Word Puzzles

4

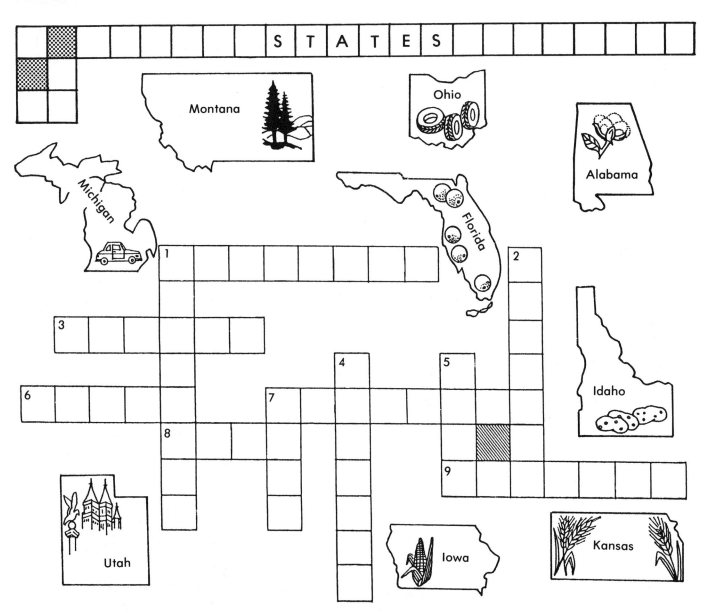

STATES

ACROSS
1. This state is far north on the Great lakes.
3. This state grows wheat and is due north of Oklahoma.
6. This state grows many potatoes and is east of Oregon.
7. This state is north of Texas.
8. This state is south of number 6 Across.
9. This state is west of Georgia.

DOWN
1. This state has a famous arch.
2. This state is in the northwestern part of the country and ends in a girl's name.
4. Oranges grow in this state which is a peninsula.
5. This state is north of Missouri and grows a lot of corn.
7. This state is east of Indiana.

Word Puzzles

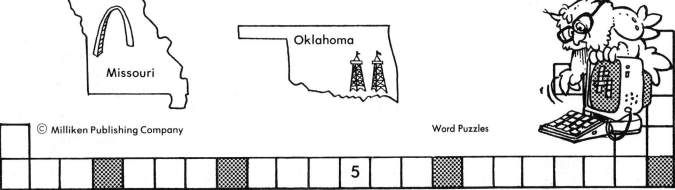

E	A	R	L	Y		N	A	T	I	V	E		A	M	E	R	I	C	A	N	

I	N	D	I	A	N	S

Fill in the blank with the correct word. Then find the words in the puzzle.

```
F  L  I  N  N  M  R  C  C  O  P
E  A  M  P  S  H  L  R  O  N  T
W  I  T  E  P  E  A  D  R  M  R
A  M  O  C  C  A  S  I  N  S  A
M  O  C  C  A  D  S  K  I  N  R
P  R  E  S  E  D  S  K  I  T  R
U  N  D  E  R  R  A  S  P  E  O
M  T  E  P  E  E  A  R  T  S  W
T  M  Y  X  L  S  P  E  A  R  S
P  A  P  O  O  S  E  R  S  E  D
```

MOCCASINS	HEADDRESS	PAPOOSE
WAMPUM	SPEAR	TEPEE
ARROWS	SKIN	CORN

1. A _____ was decorated with beautiful feathers.

2. _____ are soft slippers usually made of deerskin.

3. They lived in a tent called a _____.

4. They taught the pilgrims to grow _____.

5. _____ was used as money.

6. A baby was called a _____.

7. Most of their clothes were made from animal _____.

8. They protected themselves with bows and _____.

9. They often caught fish by using a _____.

Word Puzzles

6

THE HUMAN BODY

Fill in the puzzle blanks with the correct words.

1. Your _____ help you breathe.
2. The _____ stores food and helps digest it.
3. The _____ pumps blood to all parts of your body.
4. Your _____ helps you taste, talk, chew, and swallow.
5. An _____ helps you to hear.
6. The first _____ is below the collarbone.
7. Without your _____ , you could not think.
8. Your _____ helps you to smell.
9. You see with your _____ .
10. The _____ covers the whole body.

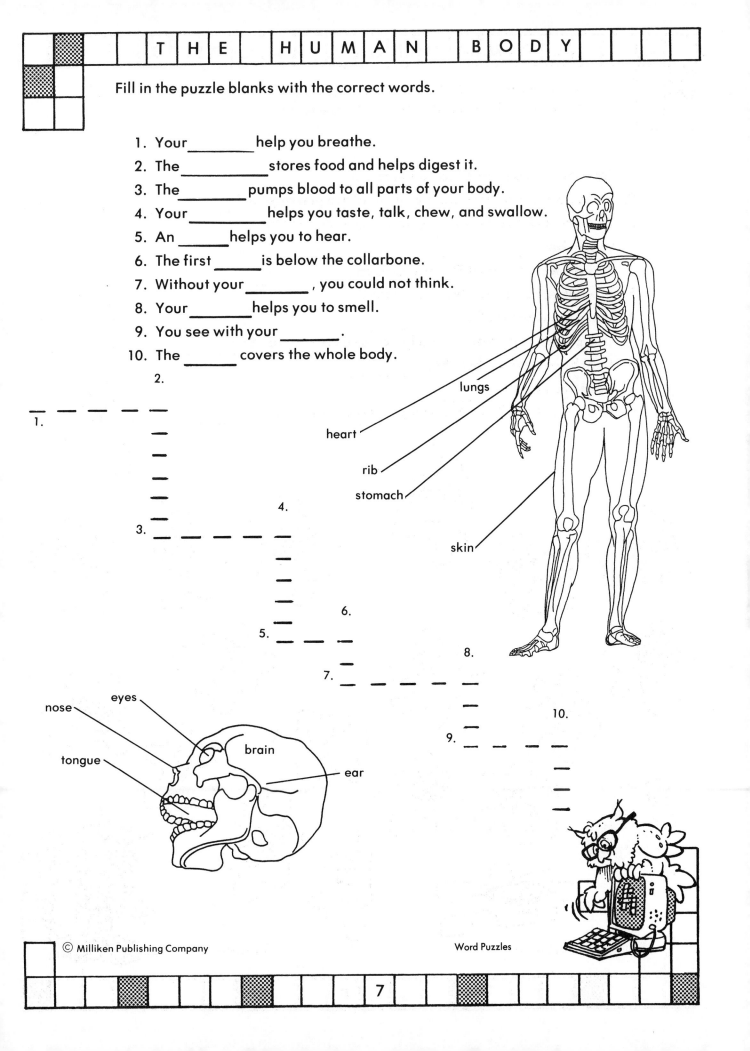

lungs

heart

rib

stomach

skin

nose

eyes

tongue

brain

ear

Word Puzzles

7

Draw a line to match the puzzle pieces to make compound words. Use these words to find the answers to the sentences.

1. This person plays on a football team. _____
2. If you pack snow into a tight ball, what are you making? _____
3. This is a book in which you write things you want to remember. _____
4. This grows in a shell under the ground. _____
5. In what game can you hit a home run? _____
6. You put a worm on this. _____
7. This person rides a horse and handles cattle on a ranch. _____
8. Most boxes are made of this. _____
9. Hogs live in this. _____
10. This is what you'll get if you stay in the sun too long. _____

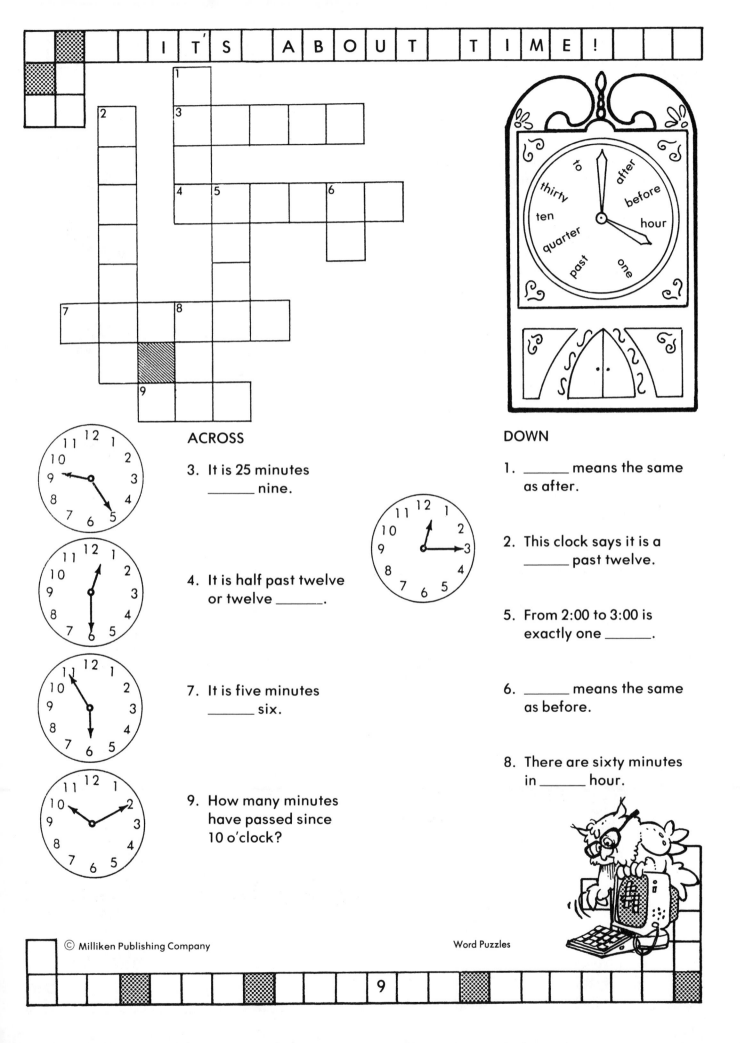

IT'S ABOUT TIME!

ACROSS

3. It is 25 minutes _____ nine.

4. It is half past twelve or twelve _____.

7. It is five minutes _____ six.

9. How many minutes have passed since 10 o'clock?

DOWN

1. _____ means the same as after.

2. This clock says it is a _____ past twelve.

5. From 2:00 to 3:00 is exactly one _____.

6. _____ means the same as before.

8. There are sixty minutes in _____ hour.

Word Puzzles

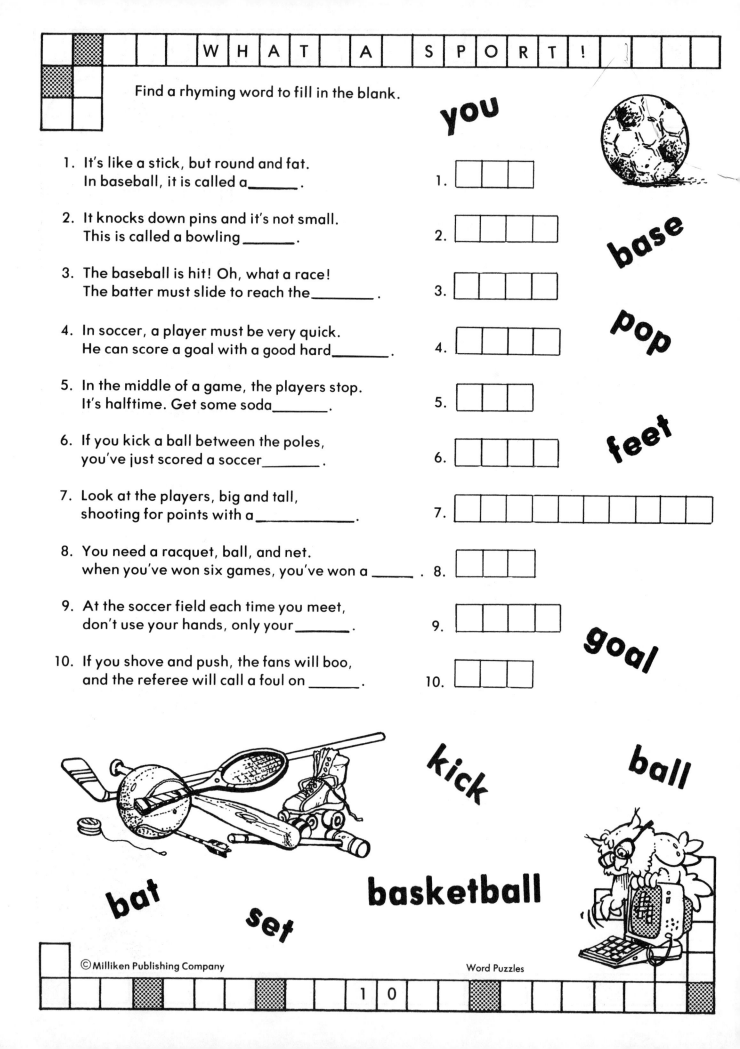

WHAT A SPORT!

Find a rhyming word to fill in the blank.

you

1. It's like a stick, but round and fat.
   In baseball, it is called a_____ .

2. It knocks down pins and it's not small.
   This is called a bowling_____ .

3. The baseball is hit! Oh, what a race!
   The batter must slide to reach the_____ .

4. In soccer, a player must be very quick.
   He can score a goal with a good hard_____ .

5. In the middle of a game, the players stop.
   It's halftime. Get some soda_____ .

6. If you kick a ball between the poles,
   you've just scored a soccer_____ .

7. Look at the players, big and tall,
   shooting for points with a_____ .

8. You need a racquet, ball, and net.
   when you've won six games, you've won a _____ .

9. At the soccer field each time you meet,
   don't use your hands, only your_____ .

10. If you shove and push, the fans will boo,
    and the referee will call a foul on_____ .

base

pop

feet

goal

kick   ball

bat

set   basketball

Word Puzzles

1 0

MAP SYMBOLS

Maps use different signs to show bridges, railroads, highways, and other things. Below you will find some of the signs used on maps. Find and circle the words in the map.

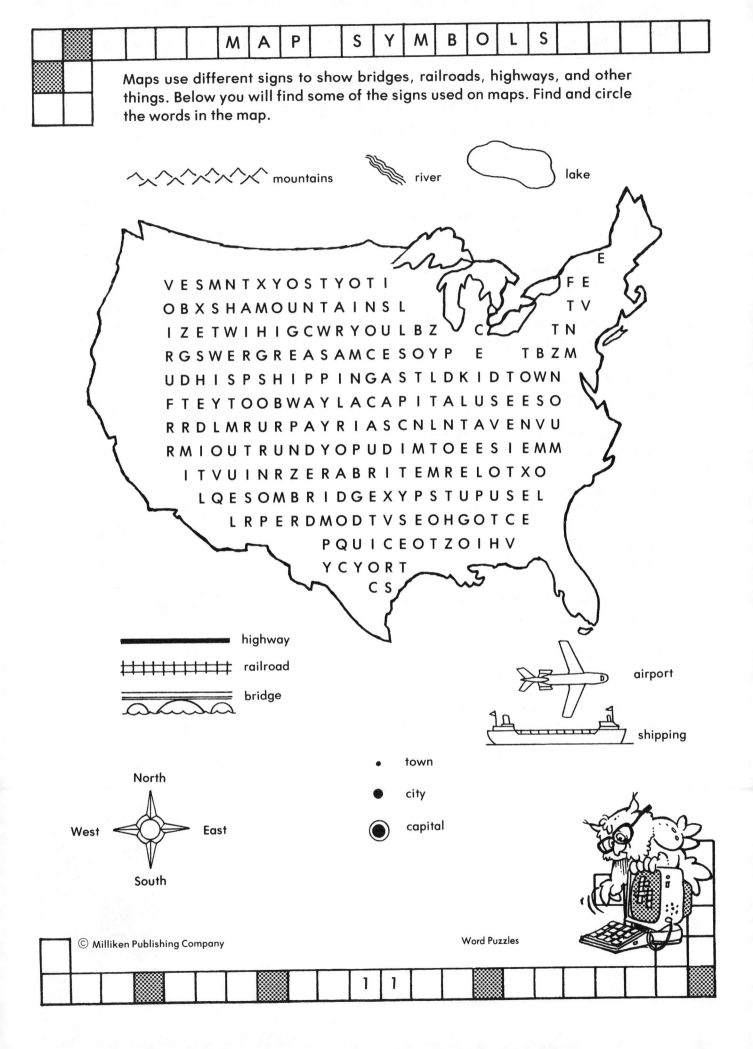

mountains   river   lake

```
V E S M N T X Y O S T Y O T I
O B X S H A M O U N T A I N S L        E
I Z E T W I H I G C W R Y O U L B Z    F E
R G S W E R G R E A S A M C E S O Y P  T V
U D H I S P S H I P P I N G A S T L D K I D T O W N    T N
F T E Y T O O B W A Y L A C A P I T A L U S E E S O    T B Z M
R R D L M R U R P A Y R I A S C N L N T A V E N V U
R M I O U T R U N D Y O P U D I M T O E E S I E M M
I T V U I N R Z E R A B R I T E M R E L O T X O
L Q E S O M B R I D G E X Y P S T U P U S E L
L R P E R D M O D T V S E O H G O T C E
P Q U I C E O T Z O I H V
Y C Y O R T
C S
```

highway

railroad

bridge

airport

shipping

town

city

capital

North

West   East

South

Word Puzzles

W	O	R	D	S		W	I	T	H		S	E	V	E	R	A	L

M	E	A	N	I	N	G	S

Look at the words and pictures on the right. Draw a line to match the picture and the words which describe it.

1. This word means to go under the water. It is also a place to wash.

2. This is the sound a dog makes and the covering of a tree.

3. This is a part of a bicycle wheel. It also means to have said something.

4. This is on the end of a finger. It is also used with a hammer.

5. This is the pair of rails on which a train runs. It also means a footprint.

6. This is something you will find on a sheet of music. It is also a short letter.

7. You can dig with this. It is also one of the suits in a deck of cards.

8. This means the highest part of something. It is also a toy that spins.

9. This is a dark place where it is not sunny. It is also a covering for a lamp.

10. This is a family of new puppies. It also means scraps and trash scattered around.

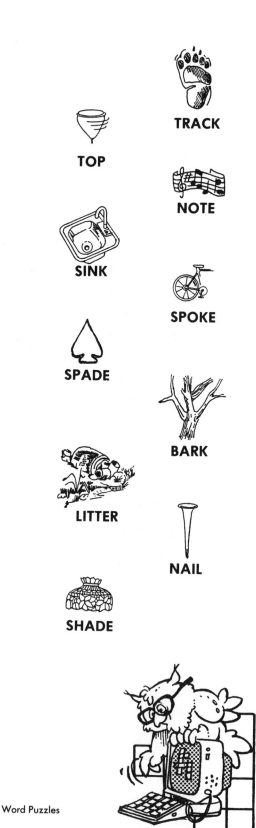

TRACK

TOP

NOTE

SINK

SPOKE

SPADE

BARK

LITTER

NAIL

SHADE

Word Puzzles

							1	2							

A N I M A L S

buffalo

giraffe

bee

penguin

frog

zebra

calf

tiger

bird

gorilla

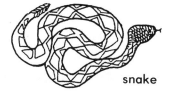

snake

DOWN

1. A _____ grows new skin several times a year.
2. A tadpole grows into a _____.
3. A _____ is a jungle cat.
4. A baby cow is a _____.
5. A _____ is an animal with feathers and wings.
6. Indians hunted the _____ for food and clothing.
9. The _____ is the largest of all apes.

ACROSS

6. A _____ makes honey.
7. A _____ is so tall he can eat leaves from the top of a tree.
8. This animal barks.
10. The _____ is a member of the horse family.
11. A _____ is a bird that cannot fly.

dog

Word Puzzles

1 3

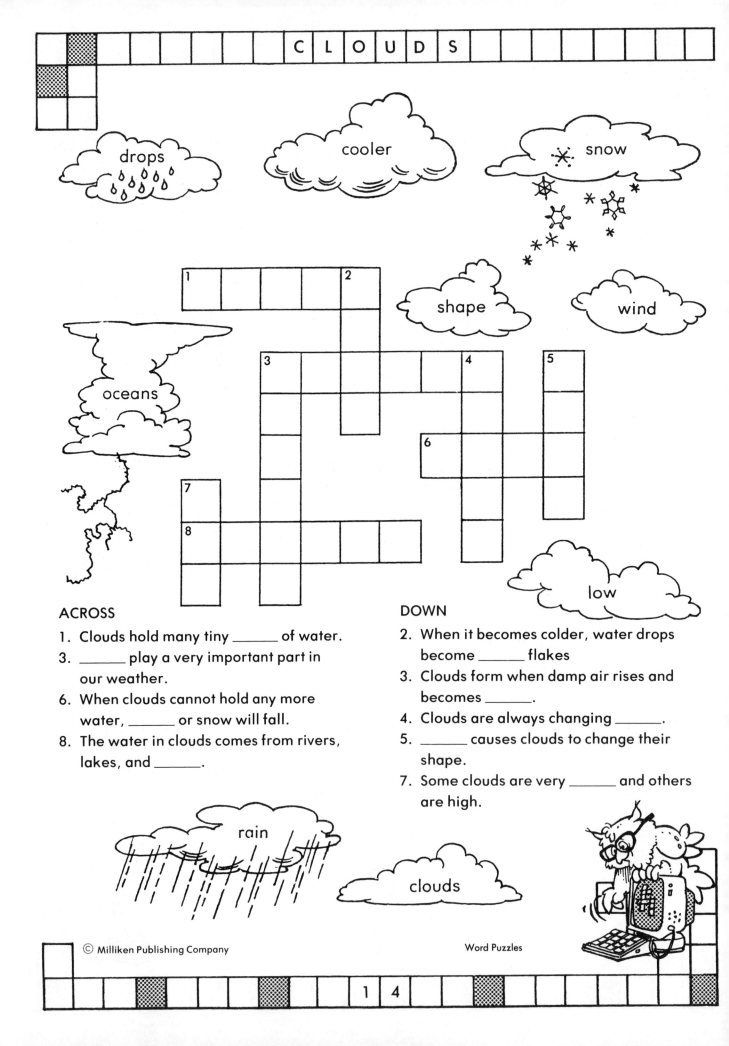

C L O U D S

ACROSS
1. Clouds hold many tiny _____ of water.
3. _____ play a very important part in our weather.
6. When clouds cannot hold any more water, _____ or snow will fall.
8. The water in clouds comes from rivers, lakes, and _____.

DOWN
2. When it becomes colder, water drops become _____ flakes
3. Clouds form when damp air rises and becomes _____.
4. Clouds are always changing _____.
5. _____ causes clouds to change their shape.
7. Some clouds are very _____ and others are high.

Word Puzzles

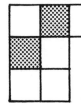
Print the first letter sound of each picture in the blank to spell a word. Then draw a line to the matching homonym.

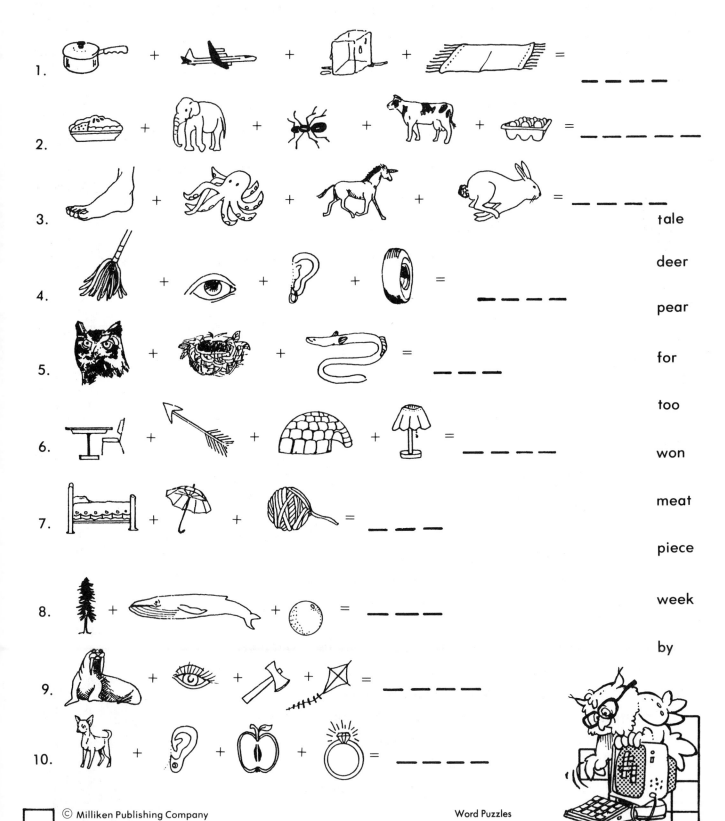

1. _ _ _ _

2. _ _ _ _ _

3. _ _ _ _

tale

deer

4. _ _ _ _

pear

for

5. _ _ _

too

won

6. _ _ _ _

meat

7. _ _ _

piece

week

8. _ _ _

by

9. _ _ _ _

10. _ _ _ _

Word Puzzles

| | | | F | A | M | O | U | S | | N | A | M | E | S | | | |

Fill in the blank with the correct name. Then find the names in the puzzle.

JEFFERSON

LINCOLN

```
T R W M F C Y T J F F R J G P N
N N J X F L P U H I O J C I O L
G F O E P L Q C Z A A K J T L H
K W H G F B R L K A S W G X O Y
G T N M J F L Q P K E N N E D Y
H I S W J E E I F I I X Z Y C U
K Z O J U E S R N H K N D X Q L
Z K N Z B G I G S F L X T Q K J
X X E P Q U O A B O X T D I G H
V U Y A F S W B C P N A K A G V
S M M Y J P T N N K P D M Q G B
P W L B E D I S O N U R X B X M
S B S K E L L E R G K Y L R F T
M S H J A L S B E E V X J S N O
V Z K U A I L Q V D Z H A R N J
```

JOHNSON

BELL

KENNEDY

WASHINGTON

EDISON

POLO

KELLER

KING

1. President Lyndon B. _____ was from Texas.
2. Alexander Graham _____ invented the telephone.
3. Thomas Alva _____ was a famous inventor who invented the telegraph.
4. There is a picture of President John F. _____ on the half dollar.
5. Marco _____ was an Italian who wrote about his travels in China.
6. Martin Luther _____ was a great black leader.
7. George _____ was the first President of the United States.
8. A picture of Abraham _____ is on the penny.
9. Helen _____ was blind and deaf.
10. Thomas _____ wrote the Declaration of Independence.

Word Puzzles

1 6

E A S Y A S P I E

Fill in the blanks with the correct letters.

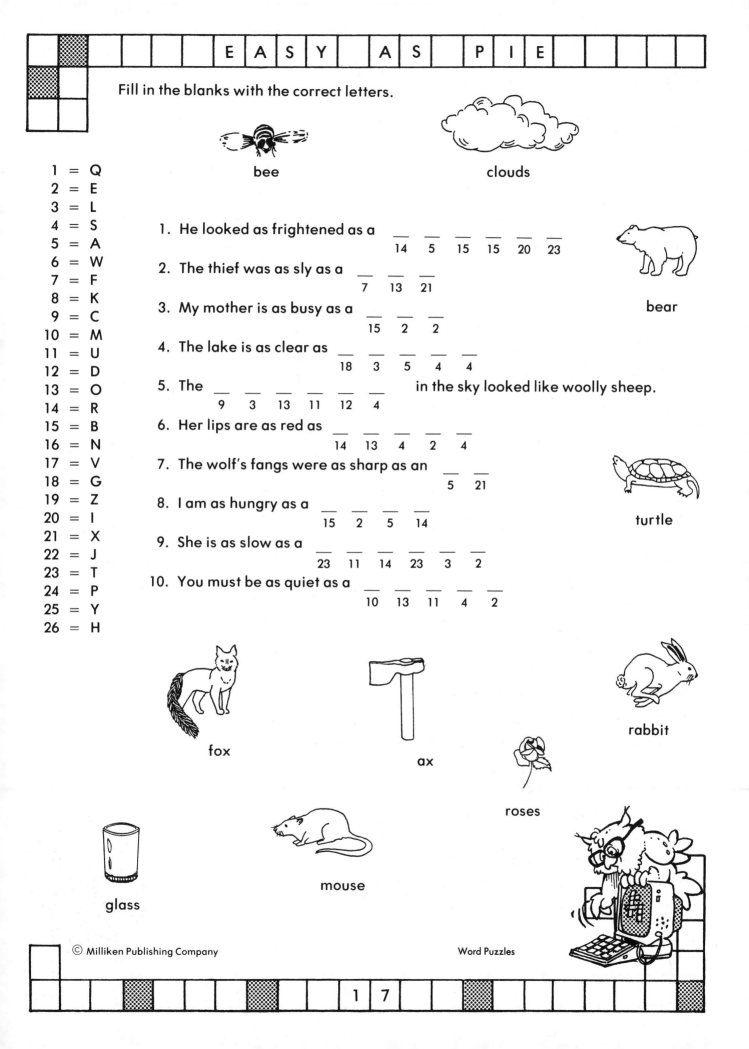

bee

clouds

bear

1 = Q	
2 = E	
3 = L	
4 = S	
5 = A	
6 = W	
7 = F	
8 = K	
9 = C	
10 = M	
11 = U	
12 = D	
13 = O	
14 = R	
15 = B	
16 = N	
17 = V	
18 = G	
19 = Z	
20 = I	
21 = X	
22 = J	
23 = T	
24 = P	
25 = Y	
26 = H	

1. He looked as frightened as a __ __ __ __ __ __
   14 5 15 15 20 23

2. The thief was as sly as a __ __ __
   7 13 21

3. My mother is as busy as a __ __ __
   15 2 2

4. The lake is as clear as __ __ __ __ __
   18 3 5 4 4

5. The __ __ __ __ __ __ in the sky looked like woolly sheep.
   9 3 13 11 12 4

6. Her lips are as red as __ __ __ __ __
   14 13 4 2 4

7. The wolf's fangs were as sharp as an __ __
   5 21

8. I am as hungry as a __ __ __ __
   15 2 5 14

9. She is as slow as a __ __ __ __ __ __
   23 11 14 23 3 2

10. You must be as quiet as a __ __ __ __ __
   10 13 11 4 2

turtle

fox

ax

roses

rabbit

glass

mouse

Word Puzzles

THE LIFE OF THE BUTTERFLY

Follow the clues carefully to complete the puzzle.

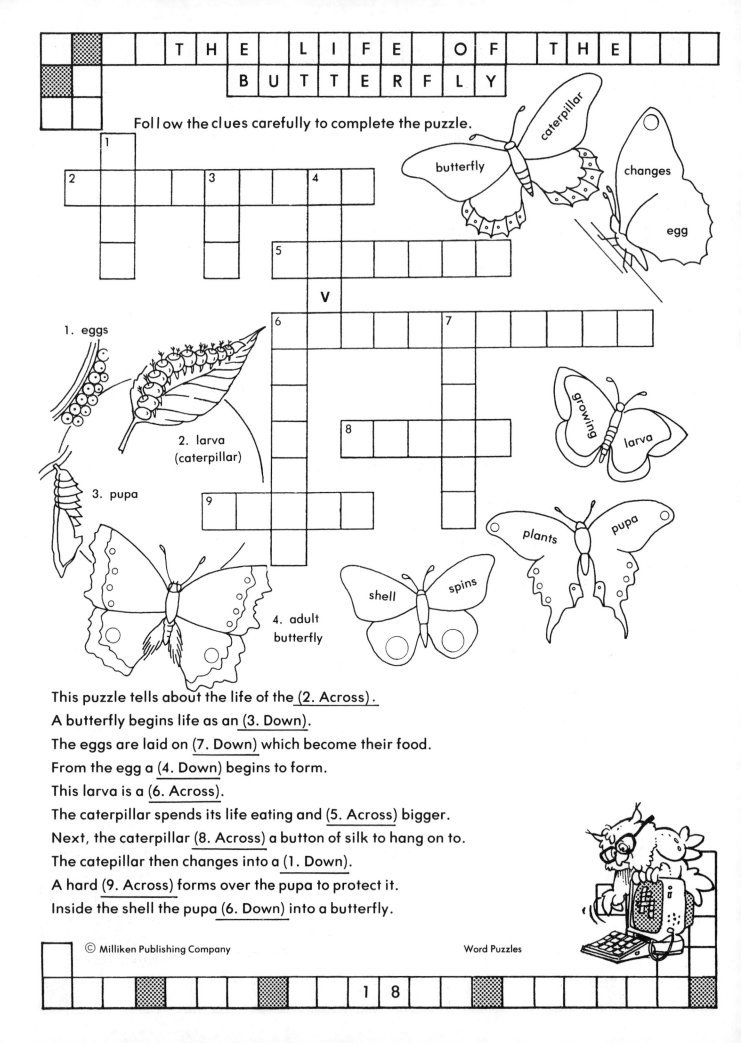

1. eggs

2. larva (caterpillar)

3. pupa

4. adult butterfly

This puzzle tells about the life of the (2. Across).

A butterfly begins life as an (3. Down).

The eggs are laid on (7. Down) which become their food.

From the egg a (4. Down) begins to form.

This larva is a (6. Across).

The caterpillar spends its life eating and (5. Across) bigger.

Next, the caterpillar (8. Across) a button of silk to hang on to.

The catepillar then changes into a (1. Down).

A hard (9. Across) forms over the pupa to protect it.

Inside the shell the pupa (6. Down) into a butterfly.

Word Puzzles

18

Find the correct word on the boats. Write it on the lines.

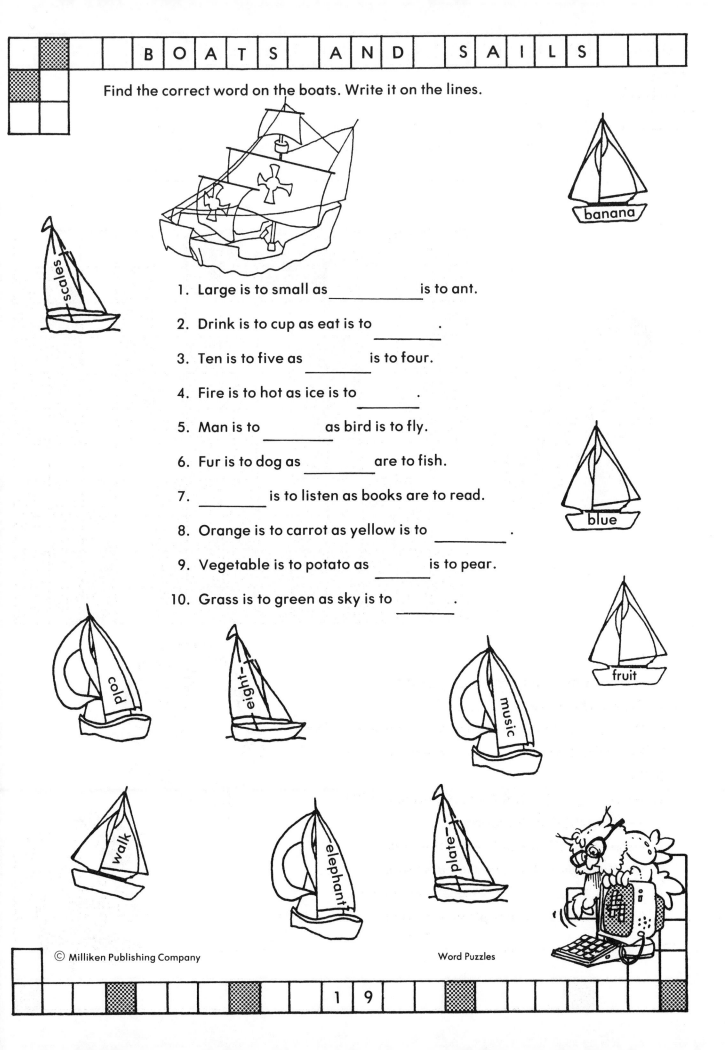

1. Large is to small as _____ is to ant.

2. Drink is to cup as eat is to _____ .

3. Ten is to five as _____ is to four.

4. Fire is to hot as ice is to _____ .

5. Man is to _____ as bird is to fly.

6. Fur is to dog as _____ are to fish.

7. _____ is to listen as books are to read.

8. Orange is to carrot as yellow is to _____ .

9. Vegetable is to potato as _____ is to pear.

10. Grass is to green as sky is to _____ .

Word Puzzles

| D | R. | | M | A | R | T | I | N | | L | U | T | H | E | R | | K | I | N | G | |

minister   peace   rights   won   black
equal   Alabama   was   schools   born

ACROSS

1. Martin Luther King was a _____ man.

4. Dr. King became a _____.

6. He _____ killed in Memphis, Tennessee in 1968.

7. He worked hard for _____ between races.

DOWN

1. He was _____ in Atlanta, Georgia in 1929.

2. Dr. King lived in Montgomery, _____.

3. He wanted all people to have the same _____.

5. Dr. King wanted children to have better _____.

6. In 1964, he _____ the Nobel Peace Prize.

8. He worked hard so people would have _____ rights.

Word Puzzles

Decode the smybols to find the synonyms.

1. hat

2. gift

3. rug

4. see

5. put

6. little

7. big

8. loud

9. sea

10. stop

11. chair

12. cup

code

a = \
b = \
c = \
d = \
e = \
f = \
g = \
h = \
i = \
j = \
k = \
l = \
m = \
n = \
o = \
p = \
q = \
r = \
s = \
t = \
u = \
v = \
w = \
x = \
y = \
z = \

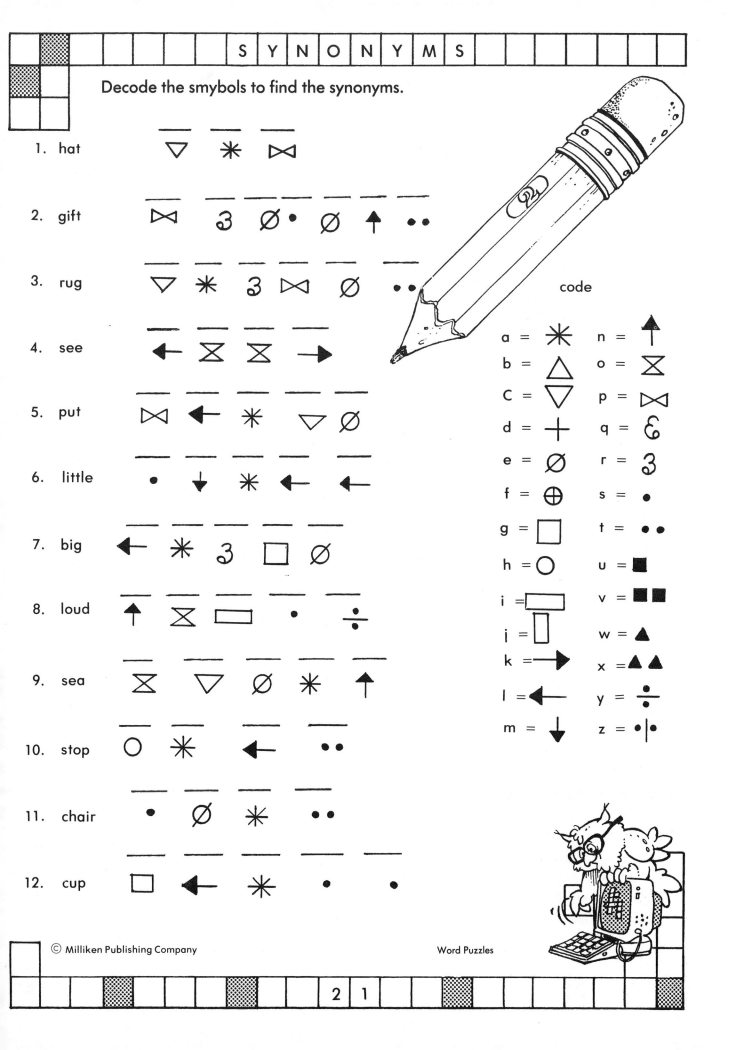

Word Puzzles

RIDDLES

Find the answers to the riddles in the puzzle.

potato

corn

```
X  R  W  Q  A  P  G  U  Y  K  D
I  A  M  K  E  X  M  F  E  P  X
D  Q  X  E  T  O  I  J  A  F  Q
Y  L  P  X  Q  E  Y  J  O  J  W
H  H  O  M  R  T  Q  J  O  J  A
H  Y  T  I  L  U  P  Z  G  L  T
V  O  A  B  N  L  Y  X  D  I  A
E  H  T  R  B  I  V  L  L  M  T
C  C  O  V  D  P  L  D  R  F  R
B  C  O  M  B  S  I  B  S  M  K
A  V  O  F  A  X  T  P  U  C  W
J  O  V  B  M  G  B  I  O  Y  E
P  R  K  M  R  H  X  L  C  K  Y
K  Y  H  I  I  B  C  L  Y  K  S
O  N  L  T  N  D  E  O  X  F  T
G  C  Y  M  I  K  J  W  G  P  H
```

pillow

tulips

yardstick

comb

chair

peep peep

clock

1. What has four legs and two arms and cannot move?
2. What has eyes and cannot see?
3. What have lips but cannot speak?
4. What has hands but cannot clap?
5. What has teeth but cannot chew?
6. What has ears and cannot hear?
7. What has three feet but cannot walk?
8. What word says the same thing backwards and forwards?
9. What has feathers but cannot fly?

Word Puzzles

2 2

P L A N E T S

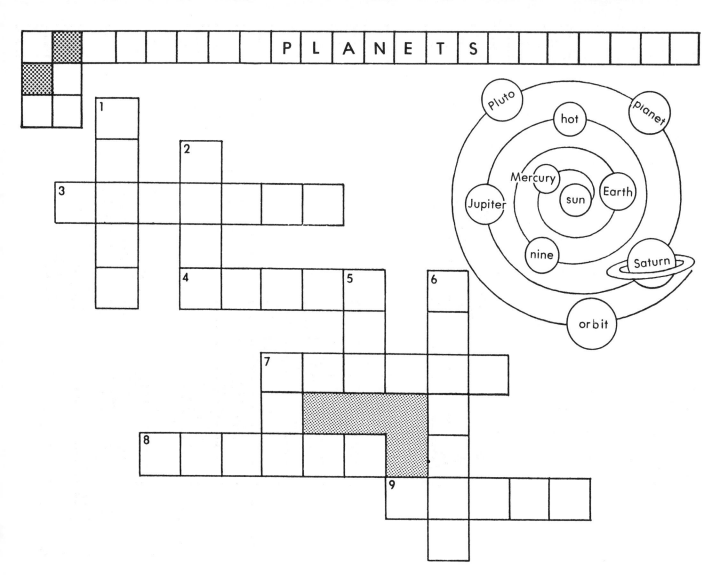

Word bank (circles): Pluto, hot, planet, Mercury, sun, Earth, Jupiter, nine, Saturn, orbit

ACROSS

3. The largest planet is _____.
4. The only planet which we know has life on it is _____.
7. The planet _____ has rings around it.
8. The sun makes its own light, but a _____ does not.
9. The planets _____ around the sun.

DOWN

1. The planet which is farthest from the sun is _____.
2. There are _____ planets in the solar system.
5. One side of Mercury is very _____ because it faces the sun.
6. _____ is the smallest planet
7. All the planets get their light from the _____.

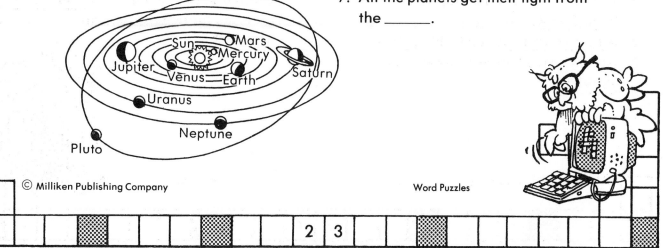

Solar system diagram labels: Sun, Mars, Mercury, Jupiter, Venus, Earth, Saturn, Uranus, Neptune, Pluto

Word Puzzles

2 3

BREAK THE CODE

Help me break the code!

A	B	C	D	E	F
1	2	3	4	5	6

G	H	I	J	K	L
7	8	9	10	11	12

M	N	O	P	Q	R
13	14	15	16	17	18

S	T	U	V	W	X
19	20	21	22	23	24

Y	Z
25	26

ACROSS

2. When you grin, you wear a 19-13-9-12-5.
3. 20-5-14-4-5-18 means gentle, kind, and loving.
6. The fuzz that you often find on clothing is 12-9-14-20.
8. The outer skin of an orange is its 18-9-14-4.
9. A 13-9-18-18-15-18 is a looking glass.
10. When you walk through water, you 23-1-4-5.

DOWN

1. A long cut or tear is a 19-12-9-20.
2. Another word for wiggle or twist is 19-17-21-9-18-13.
4. If a street is not wide it is 14-1-18-18-15-23.
5. To make smaller in size is to 18-5-4-21-3-5.
7. When you feel sleepy, you are 20-9-18-5-4.

Word Puzzles

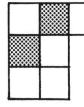

Cross out all the words with M in them.
Cross out all the words with F in them.
Cross out all the words with V in them.
Cross out all the words with K in them.

sail	ant	traffic	every	dew
smell	pale	tail	blue	moo
so	pack	ham	fresh	mew
park	sew	aunt	scent	whole
shovel	sun	ate	mask	blew
mark	hole	hare	eight	eye
heard	sale	I	fun	cent
feed	hear	tank	seven	sink
gravity	kiss	do	tale	even
plank	hair	here	son	kick
pail	far	herd	sick	over

The rest of the words make pairs of homonyms. Write the pairs on the lines.

_____   _____   _____
_____   _____   _____

_____   _____   _____
_____   _____   _____

_____   _____   _____
_____   _____   _____

_____   _____   _____
_____   _____   _____

Word Puzzles

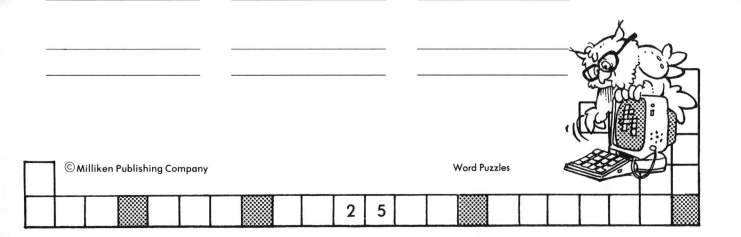

A R O U N D   T H E   W O R L D

ACROSS
1. The _____ shows us that the earth is round.
5. _____ on a map is below north.
6. East is directly opposite _____.
7. The point farthest north is the North _____.
9. A large _____ of earth is covered with water.

DOWN
2. When you move your finger from east to west, you are moving to the _____.
3. On a map, _____ is to the right of west.
4. You would find thick _____ at the North Pole.
6. Blue is used most often to show _____ on a globe.
8. On a map, north is toward the _____.
10. Many different colors are used to show _____ on a globe.

Word Puzzles

2 6

I D I O M S

Fill in the blank with the correct word. Then find the words in the puzzle.

SAD

DAYDREAM

CLUMSY

ANGRY

DIZZY

BRAVE

WATCH

TROUBLE

GARDENER

```
V  U  W  G  Y  F  J  N  B  X  Y  E  G  G
I  C  J  H  N  X  B  R  F  Z  N  Q  O  Z
F  R  M  L  M  D  I  G  Z  M  R  B  G  A
H  X  X  Q  A  Y  A  I  K  V  P  R  Z  C
W  K  L  C  P  N  D  T  T  B  D  S  H  A
E  A  S  U  J  D  G  A  R  D  E  N  E  R
Y  M  Z  M  Z  G  Y  R  Y  O  N  Z  X  D
D  D  Q  D  C  Z  O  S  Y  D  U  S  H  C
L  G  E  O  D  X  M  O  Z  K  R  B  Z  S
I  B  J  H  U  U  Y  L  Z  O  T  E  L  V
S  R  U  O  L  Q  L  Y  W  P  E  M  A  E
W  A  T  C  H  U  D  Y  P  R  M  J  U  M
V  V  D  X  H  Z  H  X  I  Q  Z  E  D  A
G  E  C  J  V  Z  Y  B  U  L  I  M  E  W
```

1. When you keep your chin up, you are being _____.
2. When you are all thumbs, you are _____.
3. When you are lightheaded, you feel _____.
4. If you have a green thumb, you are a good _____.
5. If you are in hot water, you are in _____.
6. When you blow your top, you are _____.
7. To keep an eye on the baby means to _____her.
8. If you are blue, you feel _____.
9. When your head is in the clouds, you are having a _____.

Word Puzzles

ANALOGIES

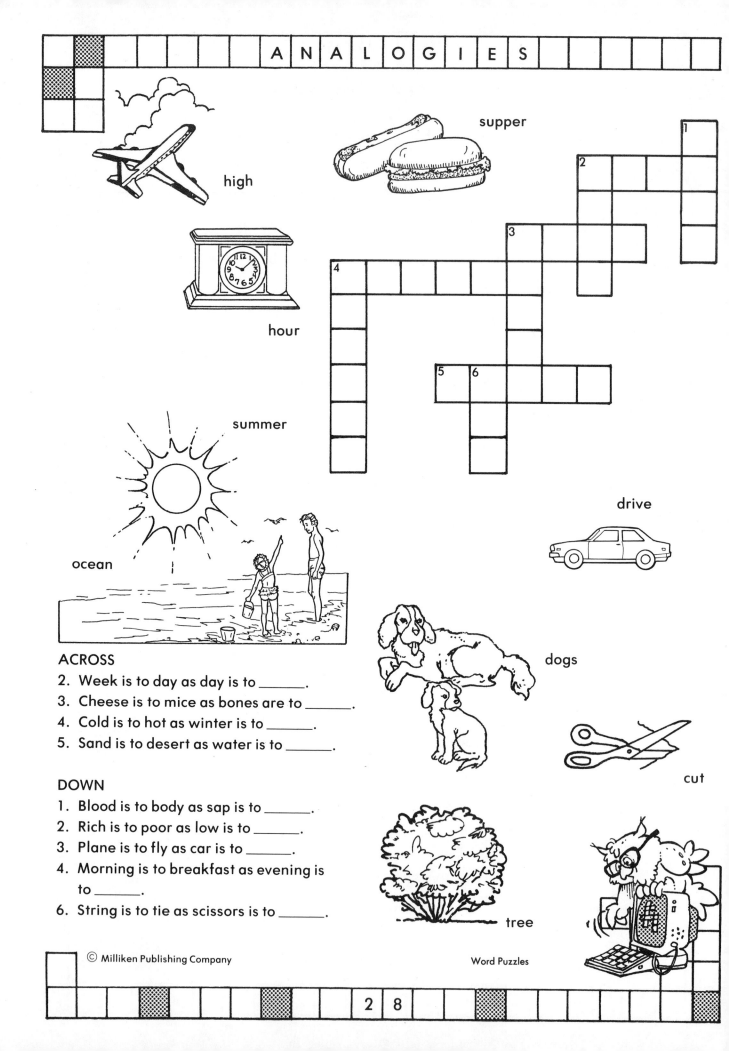

high

supper

hour

summer

ocean

drive

dogs

cut

tree

ACROSS

2. Week is to day as day is to _____.
3. Cheese is to mice as bones are to _____.
4. Cold is to hot as winter is to _____.
5. Sand is to desert as water is to _____.

DOWN

1. Blood is to body as sap is to _____.
2. Rich is to poor as low is to _____.
3. Plane is to fly as car is to _____.
4. Morning is to breakfast as evening is to _____.
6. String is to tie as scissors is to _____.

Word Puzzles

2 8